LONG ISLAND:
Picture Perfect
a photo essay

SPONSORED BY

LONG ISLAND
CONVENTION & VISITORS BUREAU
AND SPORTS COMMISSION

Produced by Island–Metro Publications, Inc.
Farmingdale, New York
631-293-6600 • www.island-metro.com

PUBLISHER *Joseph Garofalo*
PHOTOGRAPHER *Robert Lipper*
EDITOR *Nicole Sequino*
LAYOUT DESIGN *Sarah Cardullo*
AD DESIGN *Andrew Garofalo*
ADMINISTRATOR *Andrea Lombardo*
PRODUCTION *Randi Nardello-Alaggio*
ACCOUNT MANAGERS *Linda Kurtz, Gail Harrison*
ADMIN. ASSISTANT *Heather Casale*

Printed in USA   Cover Price: $21.95   ISBN: 1-888465-10-7

If you would like your own copy of

LONG ISLAND:
Picture Perfect
a photo essay

This book belongs to the hotel. Please leave it for the next guest and do not remove it from this room. If you take it home with you, the hotel will add the $21.95 cost to your bill.

However, you can order your own copy at a special price of $17.95 each (includes shipping) either by calling 631-293-6600 and charging your order to your American Express Card, or by mailing your name and address, number of copies requested and $17.95 for each copy ordered by check or money order (do not send cash) payable to Island-Metro Publications, 75 Price Parkway, Farmingdale, NY 11735. New York State residents must add appropriate sales tax, or your order will be returned.

When it comes to beauty, no place in the world can top Long Island. This long, narrow strip of land offers a vast range of unforgettable images, from endless beaches with pristine white sands that melt into the swirling blue-green waves of the Atlantic to historic homes from the Revolutionary War and the romance of the roaring 20's to craggy harbors dotted with sailboats drifting toward the horizon.

For those of us who are fortunate enough to live here, these spectacular views are part of what makes our quality of life so rich. Thanks to the photographs in this book, you can now enjoy picturesque Long Island in abundance.

All the pictures in this book were taken by Long Island travel photographer Robert Lipper of Island-Metro Publications. Many of the photos have graced the covers and inside pages of Island-Metro's various publications and calendars throughout the years, while others are new or previously unpublished photos from their collection.

Both visitors and residents will cherish this compilation of photographs of one of the most scenic and diverse spots on earth. We hope they will inspire you to find out more about Long Island and all the wonders it has to offer. We at the Long Island Convention and Visitors Bureau are awaiting your toll-free call at 1-877-FUN-ON-LI.

Michael Hollander, President
Long Island Convention and Visitors Bureau
and Sports Commission

LONG ISLAND

CONVENTION & VISITORS BUREAU
AND SPORTS COMMISSION

Discover Long Island, the Picture Perfect Place!

Looking north, looking south, looking east—gaze to any direction on Long Island and you'll find a mix of harborside and country villages, fine dining, nightlife, attractions and some of the most spectacular beaches and sunsets anywhere.

Long Island Picture Perfect takes you on a photo journey through Long Island's beaches, parklands, vineyards, farmlands, golf courses, harbors, estates, beautiful gardens, art and history museums as well as entertainment and sporting events. Tour the Gold Coast estates of yesteryear, such as the Normandy-style Falaise mansion at Sands Point Preserve and the former Phipps estate at Old Westbury Gardens, filmed in movies like Martin Scorcese's *Age of Innocence* and Alfred Hitchcock's *North by Northwest*. Drive along historic Route 25A for 40-mile journey through quaint villages, 19th-century grist mills and homes of Revolutionary War heroes. Read your favorite novel as

Springtime on the campus of S.U.N.Y. Farmingdale college.

you sunbathe or go for a swim in the Atlantic Ocean at Jones Beach or at Fire Island National Seashore, home to the Fire Island Lighthouse. Or, watch exciting thoroughbred horseracing at Belmont Racetrack, New York Islanders hockey, Long Island Ducks baseball and live entertainment on the South Shore.

Along the North Fork's winding country roads, you'll find fields, farmstands and wineries full of the season's harvest and quaint villages of antique shops and eateries on the way to Orient Point. Shelter Island, nestled between the North and South Forks, offers a serene day of bike riding, shopping and dining with harborside views. And, after visiting its fine, sandy beaches, resorts, restaurants, downtown villages and bustling nightlife, you'll learn why "The Hamptons" earns its reputation as the ultimate summer playground and leisurely autumn destination.

Take a gander through these pages and see the natural beauty, history and culture Long Island is famous for—many discoveries await you.

WHEREVER YOU ARE, WHEREVER YOU'RE GOING...

As the #1 independently owned and operated Long Island Company for over a decade, we know your neighboorhood. Serving over 300 communities, from Manhattan to Montauk.

WE CAN HELP!

RELOCATION DIVISION
1-800-237-3825 • 631-549-7480
www.prudentiallirealty.com

Prudential
Long Island Realty

(Above) The Stony Brook Grist Mill is one of many historical places to visit on the North Shore, (Right) Spring at the Temple of Love at Old Westbury Gardens, (Bottom) A winter afternoon on St. John's Pond in Cold Spring Harbor.

Historic Route 25A, also known as the North Shore Heritage Trail, stretches 40 miles from Great Neck to Port Jefferson to the quaint hamlet of Wading River. Its history dates back to 1790, when President George Washington traveled parts of this route in a horse-drawn carriage to thank his Long Island supporters and spy ring for helping to defeat the British during the Revolutionary War.

With such history, the North Shore features many Revolutionary and Civil War-period houses, history museums and grist mills. Many towns and villages

also reflect the area's history, towns like Oyster Bay, Bayville, Cold Spring Harbor, Huntington, Northport, Smithtown, Stony Brook, Port Jefferson and Wading River.

The North Shore is also known for early 1900s Gold Coast mansions and castles, charming shopping villages, fine art museums, gardens, arboretums, parks and picturesque harbors overlooking Long Island Sound. This includes Sagamore Hill National Historic Site in Oyster Bay, the "Summer White House" and Victorian mansion of President Theodore Roosevelt and his family from 1901 to 1909.

Literary greats also made their mark along the Heritage Trail. Great Neck's exquisite mansions and harbors inspired F. Scott Fitzgerald to write his masterpiece, *The Great Gatsby.* Writer Christopher Morley found solace in the Knothole, his rustic cabin in Roslyn, as did *New York Post Evening* editor William Cullen Bryant in his Cedarmere mansion. The first-published African-American poet, Jupiter Hammon, served the Joseph Lloyd Manor household in Huntington. And Walt Whitman's birthplace pays homage to the great American poet in South Huntington.

(Clockwise left page from top left) Old-fashioned candies and goods at the St. James General Store; charming Northport Village; Northport Harbor offers pristine views, even during wintertime; and the quaint village of Roslyn on an autumn day.

(Clockwise from top left) Ride the trails at the Muttowntown Preserve for an intimate view of the Island's woodlands; July 4th Celebration at Sagamore Hill National Historic Site in Oyster Bay; and tall ships at the Waterfront Festival in Glen Cove.

(Clockwise from top left) Castlegould at Sands Point Preserve; Suffolk County Vanderbilt Museum mansion; sunset sail on Long Island Sound; Dahlia gardens at Planting Fields Arboretum in Oyster Bay; and see New York's largest array of freshwater fish, reptiles and turtles at the Cold Spring Harbor Fish Hatchery.

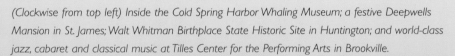

(Clockwise from top left) Inside the Cold Spring Harbor Whaling Museum; a festive Deepwells Mansion in St. James; Walt Whitman Birthplace State Historic Site in Huntington; and world-class jazz, cabaret and classical music at Tilles Center for the Performing Arts in Brookville.

(Clockwise from top left) Sunset dining in Bayville; canoeing the Nissequogue River in Kings Park; winter on the Port Jefferson waterfront; and springtime at Old Westbury Gardens.

(Clockwise from top left) Sunset on Huntington Harbor; Tranquil Clark Botanic Garden in Albertson; and Coindre Hall mansion in Huntington.

(Top) Fine and contemporary art fill the Nassau County Museum of Art in Roslyn Harbor, site of the former Childs Frick mansion.
(Bottom) Senior PGA Tour players compete at the Lightpath Long Island Classic every summer in Jericho.

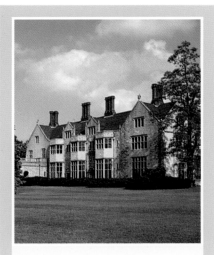

Coe Hall at Planting Fields Arboretum in Oyster Bay

Coe Hall, the Long Island Gold Coast 1920s Tudor Revival mansion of the William R. Coe family, is located on a 409 acre estate presently known as Planting Fields Arboretum State Historic Park.

The Arboretum is open daily from 10 a.m. - 5 p.m. and features sweeping lawns with majestic trees, landscape gardens, extensive greenhouse displays, educational programs and exciting horticultural activities.

For information on Planting Fields, call 516-922-9200.

Coe Hall, reflects the opulence of its time and of the William Coe family. The mansion is open daily for guided tours of restored period rooms on the first and second floors from April 1 through September 30.

For information on activities at the mansion, call 516-922-9210.

(Top to bottom) Overlooking Port Jefferson Harbor; the Charles II-style mansion at Old Westbury Gardens was home to the Phipps family in the early 1900s; and historic firetrucks, two of many horse-drawn coaches at the Long Island Museum of American Art, History & Carriages in Stony Brook.

THE SEAPORT IN FREEPORT

On the South Shore, Montauk Highway/Route 27A stretches approximately 60 miles—from Valley Stream to Shirley through small villages and seaports, with nautical museums, art galleries and shops, historic homes and picturesque views of the Great South Bay—before the road continues on to Montauk.

The region's main attraction, however, remains its miles and miles of white, sandy ocean beaches. Long Beach, one of three barrier islands that protect Long Island's mainland, harbors Atlantic Beach, Lido Beach and Point Lookout. The next barrier island includes the world-famous 2,413-acre Jones Beach State Park, which features several beachfront communities and almost 20 miles of shoreline for swimming, sunbathing and sporting events. It also contains the Jones Beach Marine Theater, one of the nation's top concert venues, as well as boardwalks, swimming pools, marinas and fishing piers.

Fire Island, the third barrier island, stretches 32 miles from Robert Moses State Park through the

Fire Island National Seashore to Smith Point County Park in Shirley. Seventeen mostly seasonal communities, some quaint and peaceful, others full of entertainment and fun, lie in between and are only accessible by passage ferry. At the end of Robert Moses, the Fire Island Lighthouse welcomes visitors to tour its 192-step tower.

The southern region also features dozens of parks, arboretums and gardens, two world-class aviation museums, amusement centers, concert halls and theaters, as well as most of Long Island's major sporting venues. This includes thoroughbred horseracing at Belmont Racetrack in Elmont, New York Islanders hockey and New York Dragons Arena Football at Nassau Coliseum, Long Island Ducks baseball at EAB Park in Central Islip and the New York Power women's soccer team at Mitchel Athletic Complex in Uniondale. And in June, 2002, the Black Course at Bethpage State Park will play host to the U.S. Open, the PGA's most prestigious golf tournament.

(Clockwise from top left) Greetings, from White Post Farms in Melville; it's down to the wire at Belmont Racetrack in Elmont; Sporting events at Mitchel Athletic Complex in Uniondale; and the Long Island Fair, complete with 1800s-style baseball, is held every October at Old Bethpage Village Restoration in Old Bethpage.

CELEBRATING **45** YEARS
OF OFFERING *more*

more

MORE OF EVERYTHING

MORE TO CELEBRATE

MORE TO REMEMBER

GREEN ACRES MALL HAS IT ALL! WITH OVER 200 GREAT SPECIALTY SHOPS, INCLUDING ANN TAYLOR LOFT, EXPRESS, MODELL'S, MEN'S WEARHOUSE AND THE CHILDREN'S PLACE, YOU'LL DISCOVER MORE OF WHAT YOU WANT. SO PENCIL US IN ON YOUR LIST OF PLACES TO SEE. BECAUSE A VISIT HERE MEANS YOU'LL NOT ONLY FIND EVERYTHING YOU WANT AND NEED, YOU'LL FIND IT IN ONE VERY CONVENIENT PLACE.

GREEN ACRES MALL
FIND GREAT SHOPPING HERE

SUNRISE HIGHWAY   VALLEY STREAM   516-561-1157   MONDAY - SATURDAY 10AM-9:30PM   SUNDAY 11AM-6PM

MACY'S   SEARS   JCPENNEY   OLD NAVY   AND OVER 200 SPECIALTY STORES

(Clockwise from top left)
Summer concerts at the Jones Beach
Marine Theater; a snowy stroll on the
Jones Beach boardwalk in Wantagh;
winter at Belmont Lake State Park in
North Babylon; and sledding is a
favorite pastime at Bethpage State
Park in Farmingdale.

Garden City Hotel in 1907

VANDERBILT MET HERE.

A millionaire sportsman who dreamed of an auto race for Long Island, William K. Vanderbilt met with friends at the Garden City Hotel to plan the first Vanderbilt Cup Race.

The hotel's handsomely appointed conference room was the perfect place to display the silver trophy, created by his friend Louis Tiffany.

The
GARDEN CITY
HOTEL

LONG ISLAND'S LEADING HOTEL
Since 1874

Garden City, Long Island, New York • 516 747-3000 • www.gchotel.com

(Top to bottom)
Long Island Ducks professional
baseball is a crowd-pleaser at
EAB Park in Central Islip;
tropical teaching garden at
Farmingdale State University;
and Jones Beach State Park
attracts millions of beach-goers
every summer.

"Oohs and aahs
are the norm at Tellers...
the stars are the steaks...
the wine list is
extraordinary".

-Joanne Starkey,
New York Times.

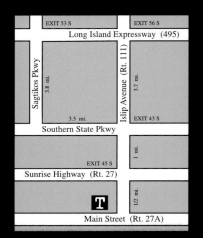

It's Prime Time.

605 Main Street, Islip
New York 11751
631.277.7070.

(Clockwise from top left) Nassau Veterans Memorial Coliseum is home to many sporting events, including New York Islanders hockey; Robert Moses State Park on Fire Island; Hofstra University's campus is an arboretum with more than 235 varieties of trees and flowers; and music, theater and comedy in an intimate theater-in-the-round format at Westbury Music Fair.

(Top) Sunset on the Great South Bay,
(Bottom) On the cycling path from
Seaford to Jones Beach.

*(Clockwise from top left)
Climb the 192-step
Fire Island Lighthouse;
harvest festivals are
abundant during Long
Island's fall season;
and dining alfresco in
Fire Island Pines.*

HOFSTRA UNIVERSITY

CONFERENCES WITH A
DEGREE OF EXCELLENCE

Plan your conference or event with a degree of excellence at **HOFSTRA UNIVERSITY.**

Conveniently located in suburban Long Island, only 25 miles east of New York City, Hofstra's beautiful 240-acre campus is a registered arboretum and nationally accredited museum, presenting more than 20 major exhibitions each year.

A conference or special event at Hofstra University offers you:

- *Reasonably priced conference facilities, accommodating groups of 10 to more than 2,000.*

- *Comfortable, air-conditioned accommodations ranging from traditional residence hall-style rooms to suites.*

- *Exceptional dining choices – from "fast food" to full service.*

- *Nine tennis courts and various playing fields.*

- *Indoor, heated, Olympic-sized swimming pool.*

Event packages include the services of an experienced coordinator to assist in each phase of the planning process and friendly, professional staff to work with your group throughout your stay at Hofstra.

For reservations or to learn more about Hofstra Conference Services call (516) 463-5067.

HOFSTRA UNIVERSITY CONFERENCE SERVICES
200 Hofstra University
Hempstead, NY 11549-2000

www.Hofstra.Edu/ConferenceServices

HOFSTRA UNIVERSITY

(Clockwise from top right)
World War II aircraft still fly at the
American Airpower Museum in Farmingdale;
Bethpage State Park's "black" golf course
will host the U.S. Open in June, 2002;
volleyball competitions in Long Beach;
and sportfishing fleet at Captree
State Park in Babylon.

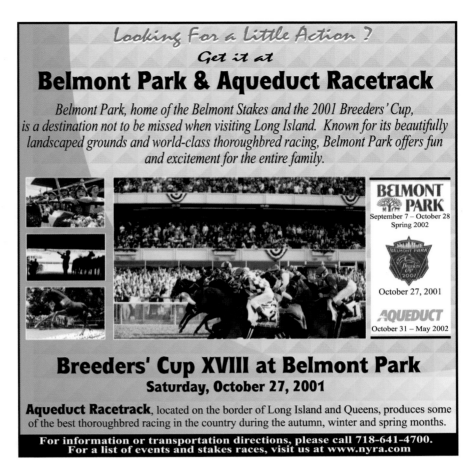

(Clockwise from top left)
Hiking path at Bayard
Cutting Arboretum in
Oakdale; a frozen State
Channel along Ocean
Parkway in Babylon;
watersports at Heckscher
State Park in East Islip;
and autumn's colors
prevail at farmstands
across Long Island.

(Clockwise from above) Serene splendor in East Marion; roadside produce in Aquebogue; pick-your-own at Krupski's Pumpkin Farm in Peconic; and harvest festivities in farm country.

THE NORTH FORK

Throughout the year, many escape to the North Fork for quiet, scenic drives past small villages, farms and wineries on Sound Avenue/Route 48 and Main Road/Route 25.

While the summer season bustles with strawberry, peach and vegetable picking, the North Fork emerges a spectacular red, orange and gold sight in autumn. Many out-of-towners go apple and pumpkin picking, or visit corn mazes, haunted houses and fall festivals.

Your East End journey starts in Riverhead on Route 58, where farmlands give way to the huge Tanger Outlet Center and the town's many popular attractions, including a historic farm, railroad museum, Long Island's only NASCAR racetrack and art galleries.

The summer haven, Splish Splash Water Park, features a wave pool, lazy river and 17 water slides. Main Street provides a serene day of shopping, museum visits and a tour of Atlantis Marine World, Long Island's first aquarium.

Route 58 soon turns into Main Road/Route 25 and takes you through Aquebogue, Laurel, Mattituck, New Suffolk, Cutchogue, Peconic, Southold, Greenport, East Marion, and, finally, Orient. Each of these villages offer a relaxing day amid roadside farmstands, antiques shops, boutiques, whaling and history museums, luncheonettes and restaurants. Seventeen wineries dot Main Road/Route 25 and Sound Avenue/Route 48, many offering tours and tastings of the season's best and live music on weekends.

(Clockwise from left) Autumn colors on the Peconic River in Calverton; apple picking in Riverhead; the Long Island Railroad Museum has two locations—one in Riverhead (pictured) and the other in Greenport; and hard-to-find items in Jamesport.

(Right) Indian Island Golf Course overlooking the Peconic River. (Below) Run through the cornfields in Mattituck; and a great view from Shelter Island, only accessible by boat or ferry.

(Clockwise from top) Canoeing the Peconic River in Calverton; shark tank at Atlantis Marine World in Riverhead; cooling off at Splish-Splash Water Park in Riverhead; and the Peconic River Herb Farm in Calverton.

(Clockwise from top left) Palmer Vineyards is one of 21 wineries on the North Fork; sunset surfcasting in Greenport; and summer harvest in Cutchogue.

LOCAL Blueberries 3.50 pt.
LOCAL Peaches 3.00 qt.
CALIFORNIA STRAWBERRIES 2.75 pt.

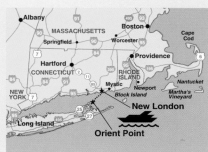

LOOKING
EAST

THE SOUTH FORK

Apart from the glitz and glamour, this region known as "The Hamptons," offers more than trendy nightclubs and its reputation an elite haven for the wealthy and famous.

The South Fork's eleven villages from Eastport to Montauk Point charm visitors with their sophisticated shops, award-winning restaurants, history museums and art galleries, theaters, chic antique stores and even several windmills. The region stretches for 50 miles with white, sandy ocean beaches, noted as some of the best in the world for their seclusion, sporting competitions, sandcastle contests and picturesque beauty. Many beaches are lined by opulent mansions and exclusive resorts, others are surrounded by high dunes and bluffs, and one is home to a famous lighthouse.

Traveling along the main road, Montauk Highway/Route 27A, the first of three South Fork wineries emerges, followed by two others in Bridgehampton and Sagaponack. Pick-your-own farms and roadside farmstands offer strawberries and vegetables in the summer, and apples and pumpkins during the fall harvest. Many parks, hiking trails, harbors, horseback riding paths and popular fishing areas mark the entire South Fork, denoting the Hamptons' natural beauty and pristine wilderness.

Sporting events are also favored by Hamptons locales and visitors. The Shinnecock Golf Club in Southampton, the oldest private 18-hole golf course in the nation, will host the 2004 U.S. Open, while Montauk Downs State Park in Montauk earned a spot among the nation's top 50 public golf courses in *Golf Digest Magazine*. Bridgehampton Polo Club Matches, the Cartier Grand Slam VII Tennis Tournament and the Hampton Classic Horse Show also complement the Hamptons' huge list of sporting events.

Unique to the Hamptons, Sag Harbor earns its fame as the area's 300-year-old fishing and whaling port. Its maritime heritage remains among the yachts and sailboats found along the Long Wharf. And, at Long Island's easternmost tip, the 80-foot Montauk Point Lighthouse sits at Montauk Point State Park as the oldest operating lighthouse in New York State.

(Pictured left, top to bottom) Old Hook Mill in East Hampton; Main Street shopping in Southampton; and Sagpond Vineyards in Bridgehampton.

(Pictured right) Downtown Westhampton Beach; and all paths lead to the beach on Dune Road.

Photo by Eleanor Labrozzi

(Clockwise from top left)
Montauk Lighthouse at the
easternmost tip of Long
Island; Hampton Classic
Horse Show in
Bridgehampton; the
landmark Big Duck in
Flanders; horseback riding on
Montauk's beaches; strolling
the Hamptons beaches; and
birdwatching on Peconic Bay.

(Pictured at right)
Wildflowers on the
beach in Montauk; and
Waldbaum's Balloon Festival
at Brookhaven-Calabro
Airport in Shirley.

(Clockwise from left) Sag Harbor Whaling Museum; sandcastle contest in Amagansett; the many faces of winter at the Parrish Art Museum in Southampton; reflections of summer in Westhampton Beach; and roadside farmstand in Bridgehampton.